The WESTERN RAILROADER
For the Western Railfan

Monterey & Pacific Grove car 21 in the Monterey Presidio about 1907 at the Ord Barracks.—Erle C. Hanson collection.

MONTEREY & PACIFIC GROVE RAILWAY

VOL. 22, NO. 10   SEPTEMBER, 1959   ISSUE 238

Monterey & Pacific Grove Railway car 21 at Southern Pacific Pacific Grove depot. Rudolph Brandt Collection

Monterey & Pacific Grove Railway car 18 on Lighthouse Avenue, Pacific Grove, September 20, 1907.
M. B. Collection courtesy R. Brandt

Monterey & Pacific Grove Railway

By ERLE C. HANSON

One hundred eighteen miles south of San Francisco lies the picturesque city of Monterey. Historically famous as California's first state capital, having the first theater in the state, and for its many adobe missions and state landmarks that may still be seen, Monterey also had a colorful history connected with its local street railway system. From 1890, until its abandonment in 1923, the Monterey & Pacific Grove Railway ran between the towns of Pacific Grove (the Chautauqua of California), Monterey, and the Hotel Del Monte, in Del Monte. Starting out as a narrow gauge horsecar line on August 12, 1890, when Juan Malarin and his associates, L. C. Allen and M. V. McQuigg were granted the right under city ordinance No. 27 to lay narrow gauge (3' 2") tracks on certain city streets. This was signed by T. J. Field, chairman of the board of supervisors. The line would be of single track for its entire length, having passing tracks at intervals. Commencing in Pacific Grove (known to the old timers of the area as "The Grove") on Lighthouse Ave. and 17th St. and continuing along Lighthouse, Fountain, Central, private right-of-way, Lighthouse to Decator St. in Monterey, then to Alvarado, Munras, Pearl, Washington, to Perry St. (Del Monte Ave.), and on to Ocean Ave. through the beautiful tree bordered streets of Oak Grove, to 7th St. and to the west gate of the Del Monte Hotel grounds at Sloat Ave.

A car barn was built at the Del Monte terminus and also on Central Ave. at 2nd St. in Pacific Grove. Malarin had big ideas for his coming street railroad and ordered 10 new double end horsecars from Fitzgerald Company in San Jose. With his accustomed energy and push, Malarin rushed the final work to completion in August. The cars arrived, received last minute preparations and were numbered 1-10 inclusive. On August 5, 1891, service was officially started. Each car was drawn by two horses, and soon became a familiar sight on the city streets. The cars were trimmed in apple green and yellow.

The road continued to operate with great success and on June 3, 1893, the company was re-organized under the name Monterey & Pacific Grove St. Ry. & Electric Power Co. This increased the number of directors from five to seven. H. A. Greene took over the position as president; Juan Malarin as secretary. Though cars rarely ran on schedule, the road was satisfactory as an investment, for from the outset it declared regular dividends to its stockholders.

In the fall of 1902, plans were made to electrify the entire system. Without question, the greatest factor in the building of Monterey and Pacific Grove was the conversion of the old horsecar line between the two cities into a modern electric street railroad. L. C. Allen was appointed as manager; F. M. Hilby became vice-president. The name remained unchanged and new electric cars were ordered from the St. Louis Car Co., in addition to the 10 horsecars that were rebuilt into single truck electric cars.

The original narrow gauge track was retained as the roadbed was in excellent condition. The only changes in the route were in downtown Monterey where new rails were laid from Munras to Webster, Figueroa, and Perry St. (Del Monte Ave.), and on Lighthouse Ave. between Decator and Alvarado St. The routes on Pearl, Washington and Decator St. were abandoned. In addition to rebuilding the suburban line between Del Monte and the Grove, a crosstown line was built from the S.P. depot at Perry and Adams St. via Adams, Franklin, to and into the Monterey Presidio, known as Ord Barracks. Work was completed in August, 1903, on both lines and revenue service was started, using the rebuilt cars which retained their original numbers of 1-10 inclusive. These cars were mounted on a Stephenson single truck, powered by two 25 h.p. Walker motors, equipped with two "J" controllers and were trimmed in maroon and gold gilt. A large car house-power station was built on Figueroa and Perry St. and 600 volts D.C. was used to power equipment. The old Del Monte horsecar barn was retained for the electrics, but the Pacific Grove barn was abandoned.

During the spring of 1904, eight new double truck cars arrived from the St. Louis Car Co. Four were open summer cars and four were combination half open, half closed (California type). The open cars were 30 feet in length and the combinations were 34 feet. Both were equipped with two 25 h.p. G.E. motors, two "K" controllers and wire safety fenders. They were numbered open cars 11-14, combination (California type) 16-19 inclusive. A single truck line car was built at the Monterey barns and numbered 13. All cars were fitted with the Ohmer register. These registers recorded the number of passengers carried, number of five and ten-cent fares, school tickets, transfers, etc., collected by the conductor, also the trip and the mileage made by the car aaily. The fare between Del Monte and the Grove was set at 20 cents, to Monterey only was 10 cents, and five cents on the Ord Barracks line. A fifteen minute service was provided on both lines and in June, 1904, the fare between Del Monte and the Grove was reduced to 10 cents. Ticket books could be purchased which entitled one to ride half fare, thus giving regular patrons the benefit of a five cent fare over the whole road.

In 1905, the entire road was standard gauged (4' 8½") and the rebuilt cars, 1-10 inclusive, were equipped with SP rebuilt double trucks. All of the rebuilt cars were lengthened to 25 feet. Numbers 1-5 inclusive were renumbered 22-26 inclusive. Numbers 6-10 inclusive became 15, 20, 21, 27, and 28.

Forty-five pound steel rails were used on the entire line. Shortly before completion the company was taken over by the Byllesby Syndicate Co. of Chicago (the same syndicate that controlled the United Railroads of San Francisco). Original plans were retained by these new owners, the M&PG Ry. kept its name and an extension to the SP depot in the Grove was built from Lighthouse Ave. and 17th St. along Lighthouse Ave. and 19th St. to

One of the original horsecars of the Monterey & Pacific Grove Railway at the S.P. depot in Monterey at Adams and Perry Streets about 1903.—Hanson collection.

Two M&PG cars passing on Lighthouse Avenue at Decator Street passing track with the Monterey waterfront in the background about 1905.—Hanson collection.

The Del Monte terminus carbarn with car 15 about 1907.

The power house at Adams and Perry Streets in Monterey about 1905 with car 21 passing on Perry. The building is still in use as a Pacific Gas & Electric substation and warehouse.

Car 21 starts down the Franklin Street grade to Monterey from the Presidio about 1908.—Lorrin Silleman collection.

Car 19 in front of the Hotel El Carmelo at Fountain and Lighthouse in Pacific Grove about 1909.

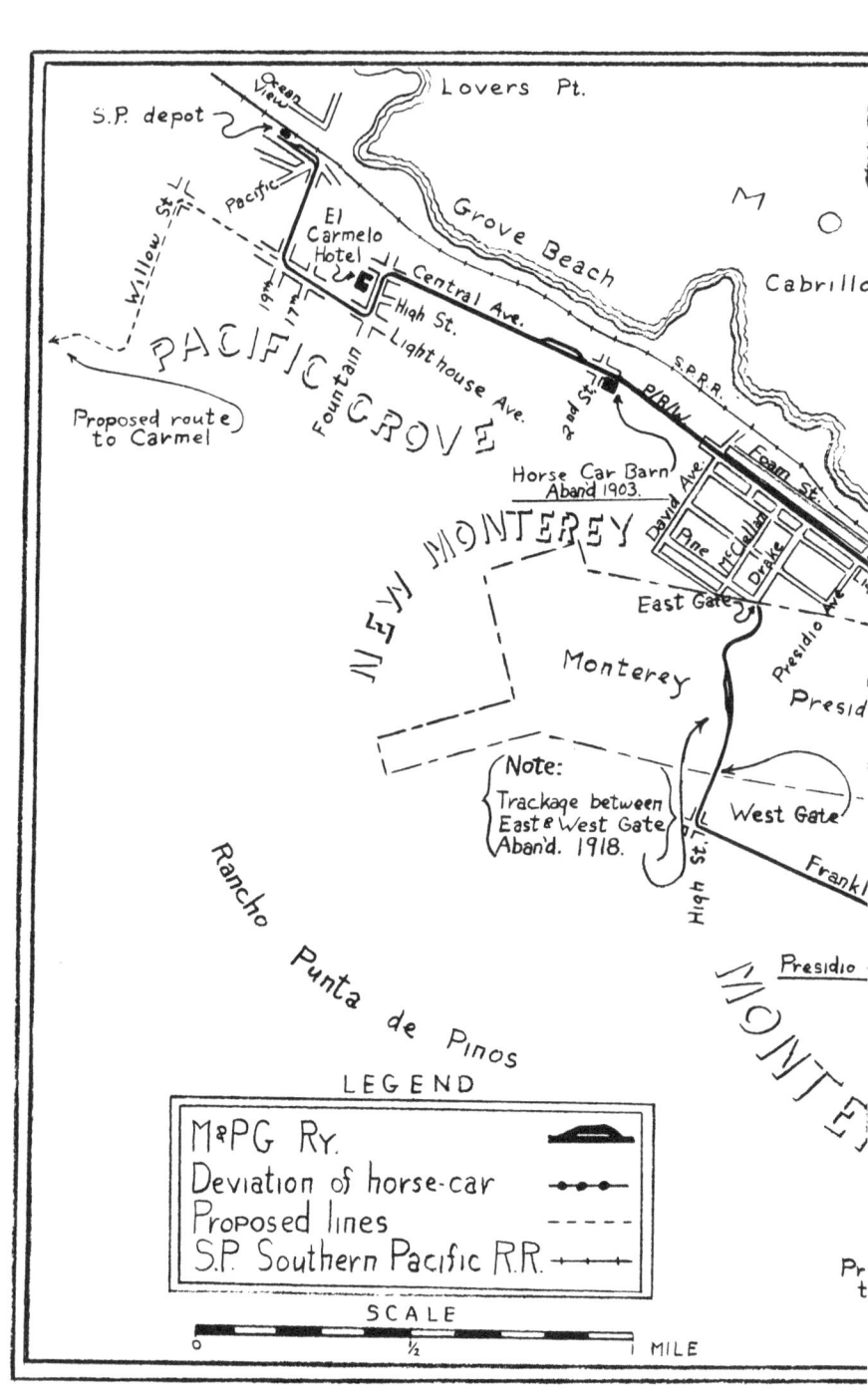

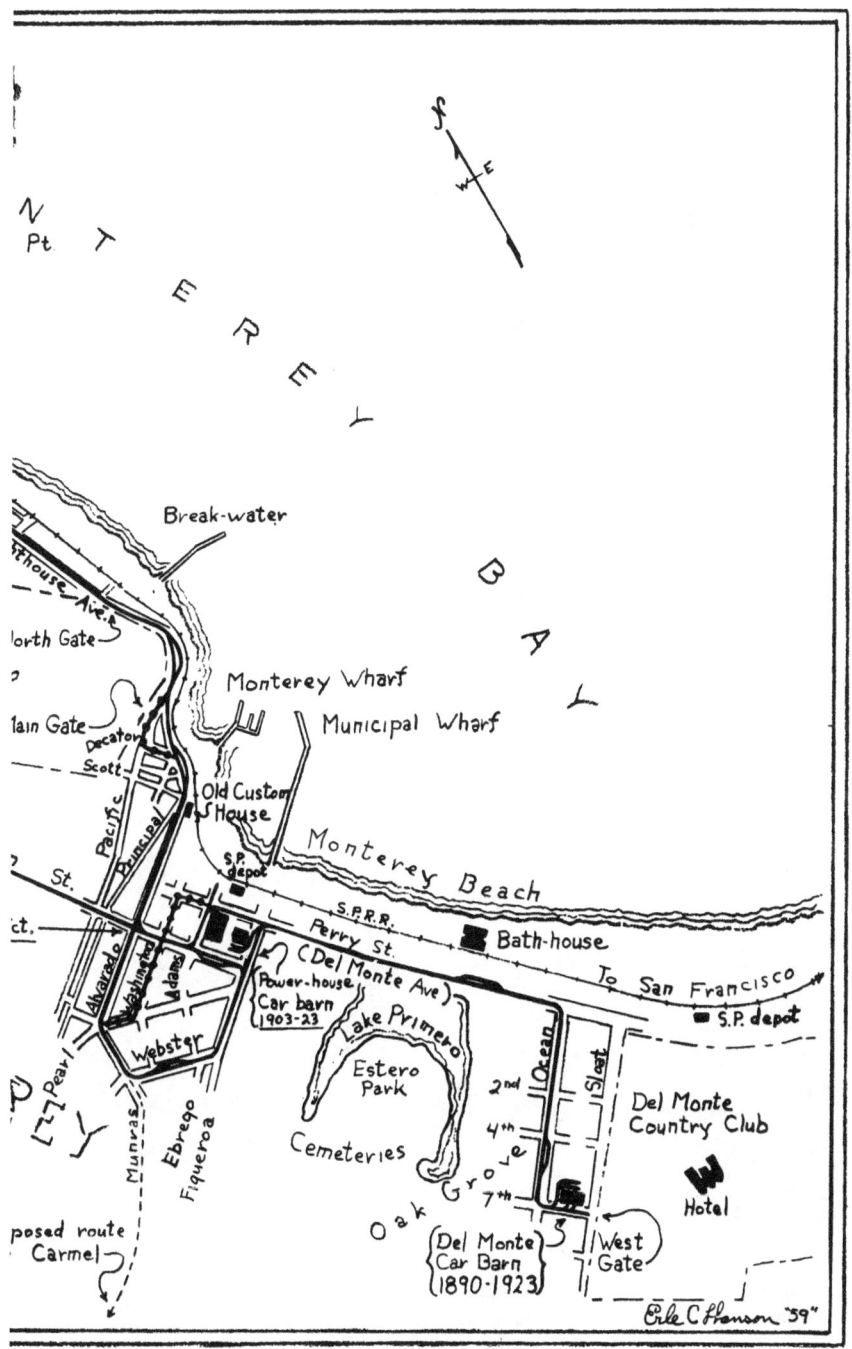

One of the rebuilt horsecars on electric trucks about 1905 at the Pacific Grove S.P. depot.—Ken Kidder.

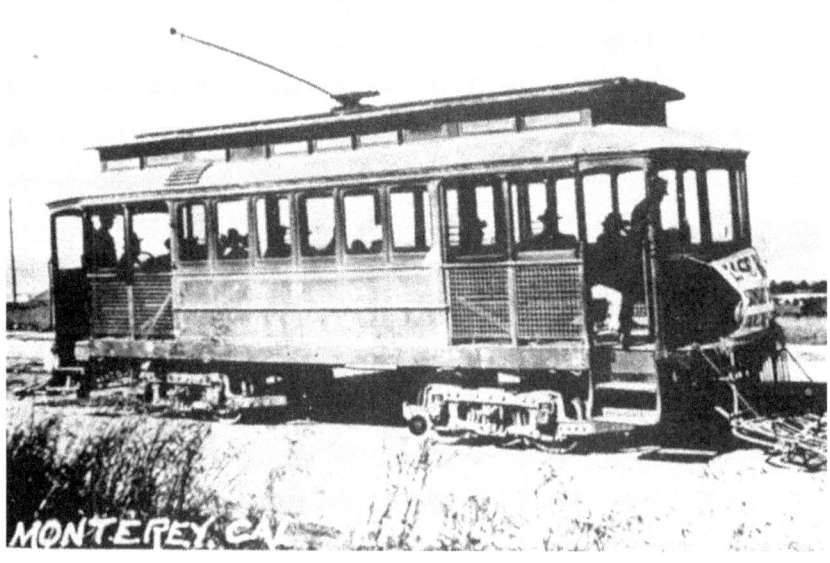

M&PG car 3 rounds the bend on Lighthouse Avenue near the beach and Municipal Wharf on September 12, 1920. Photo by L. Slevin from the Roy D. Graves collection.

M&PG car 4 stops at the Custom House on Alvarado Street in Monterey on Sept. 12, 1920. Photo by L. Slevin from the collection of Roy D. Graves.

M&PG car 8 on Franklin Street at Alvarado in Monterey in September, 1920. Photo by L. Slevin from the collection of Roy D. Graves.

M&PG car 5 in front of the Pacific Grove Methodist Church on Lighthouse at 17th Street in September, 1920. Photo by L. Slevin from the collection of Roy D. Graves.

M&PG car 15 on Lighthouse Avenue in downtown Pacific Grove about 1920. Wilbur C. Whittaker collection.

the depot. Fifty pound steel rails were used on this extension.

In May, 1905, the entire system was open to revenue business. Chief Engineer Ira B. Funk, who supervised the standard gauging of the line, acted as motorman on one of the new St. Louis closed cars loaded to capacity with such company notables as M. V. McQuigg, L. C. Allen, R. C. P. Smith, newly appointed treasurer, and J. M. Gardener of Santa Cruz. This special trip was without a doubt a successful one and many of the out-of-town notables were quoted as saying, "It is without a doubt one of the grandest scenic roads on the Pacific coast."

In addition to the regular suburban line from Del Monte to the Grove, two runs were operated to Monterey only. The first, entering Monterey from Del Monte via Perry St. to Adams, to Franklin, to Alvarado St. and returned to Del Monte. The second run entered Monterey from Pacific Grove on Alvarado St. and looped via Munras, Webster, Figueroa, Franklin, to Alvarado St., and returned to the Grove. Additional passing tracks were installed along the line to accommodate the added runs.

Plans were made to construct an extension from Pacific Grove, on Lighthouse Ave. and 19th St. The road would proceed on Lighthouse Ave. to Willow St., and via Willow St. to the street's end, where private right-of-way would parallel the famous "Seventeen Mile Drive" along the beautiful Pacific Ocean to Carmel. Then it would continue through the picturesque Carmel Valley to Monterey where the line would connect with the Del Monte line on Munras at Webster St. This projected line, for an unknown reason, was never started.

During the fall of 1905, a parlor car was ordered from the St. Louis Car Co. and was received late in 1905. This car was a superb product of the car builders art. It was 36 feet in length, and fitted with every possible convenience and luxury. The windows were extra large, the interior was of rare imported mahogany fixtures, and the draperies were of fancy silk and plush. At each end was an open observation section, enclosed with grill work of solid bronze three feet in height. The car was trimmed in the company colors and was named "Del Monte." Two K-1 controllers were fitted at each end and four G.E. 70 motors mounted on two St. Louis 23-A trucks were used. At first the car was used only on special inspection trips over the road, but in later years it served as the famous sight-seeing car operating between Del Monte and the Grove with a specially installed gramaphone that played "In Old Monterey," as its passengers enjoyed the scenic ride over the, then called, "Bay Shore Line."

Between the years 1906-15, the areas lying between Del Monte and the Grove had expanded their population. Farms, resorts and new improved streets, the private automobile and jitney service was felt by the M&PG Ry. Cars 11-14 inclusive were demotorized and used as trailers behind the St. Louis cars during peak hours, weekends, and on special occasions. The installation of a wye at each terminus was not necessary as the motor cars could take the lead by means of a passing track.

Special dances and other attractions were staged by the M&PG Ry. to help aid the declining passenger revenue. With the outbreak of World War I, the Presidio of Monterey was suddenly presented with thousands of new recruits. Almost overnight, the pas-

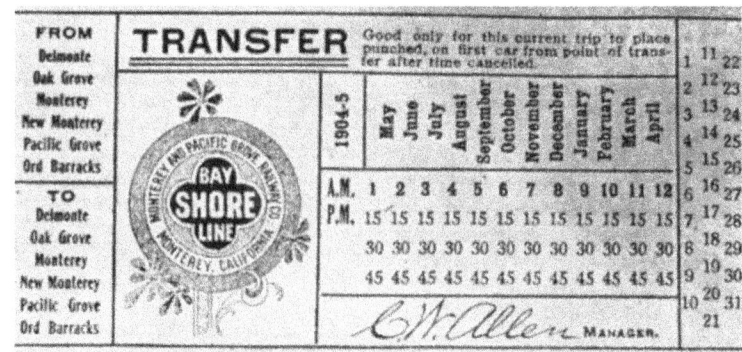

THE MONTEREY AND PACIFIC GROVE RAILWAY COMPANY'S UNIVERSAL TRANSFER

senger revenue hit an all-time high on the M&PG, and though only one car was regularly used on the single track Ord Barracks line, as many as five cars were seen challenging the steep grade up Franklin St. hill each in turn loaded to capacity with many soldiers of the 11th Cavalry. During the war years a civilian was lucky to get a seat on a car after a Saturday night dance let out at the Del Monte Bath House, or at the beach in the Grove. The fare remained at 10 cents on the Bay Shore Line and five cents on the Ord Barracks and split suburban lines. With the signing of the armistice of World War I, many of the city's war-time residents returned to their respective home lands, a few established permanent residence, but the M&PG's passenger revenue dropped to pre-war levels. Trailers 11-14 inclusive were housed at the Del Monte car barns, then used as a boneyard for retired and wrecked equipment. The Ord Barracks line was terminated at the east gate of the Presidio where the dirt road had been paved, as were all the streets in Monterey at this time. It was named High St. The sightseeing parlor car, "Del Monte," continued its familiar tours until 1920, when it was taken out of service and housed at the Monterey car barn until sold to a private owner in Los Gatos, where it remained as a private home until destroyed by fire in 1945.

In 1918, the entire fleet of M&PG cars were completely renumbered. Cars 11-14 inclusive were motorized, closed and renumbered 5-7 and 9. Nos. 16-19 inclusive became 1-4, and 20 and 24 became 8 and 10. Cars 15, 21, 22, 23, 25, 26, 27, and 28 were scrapped at the Del Monte car barn. The maroon paint scheme was retained.

Twenty minute headways were operated on the Bay Shore Line with 10 minute layovers at each terminus. A 30 minute schedule was used on the Ord Barracks line, then known as the Franklin St. line. In 1923, the M&PG Ry. applied for permission to abandon its entire system, and on July 20, 1923, service was discontinued. All equipment was scrapped at the Del Monte car barns and then the barns were torn down. The Mon-

Monterey & Pacific Grove car 5 on Alvarado Street in Monterey. From the collection of Kenneth Kidder.

terey car barn was torn down also, but the power house was retained as a warehouse for the Monterey County Gas & Electric Co., and is still used today by the PG&E Co. The only traces of the old M&PG Ry. are the poorly patched parallel scars on 19th St. where the line executed a graceful curve on the approach to the Pacific Grove SP depot. The city of Monterey was indeed indebted to the M&PG Ry. for its part in helping to bring the neighboring communities together.

Copyright 1959 and 1967 by Erle C. Hanson - F.A. Guido

THE WESTERN RAILROADER
"FOR THE WESTERN RAILFAN"
P.O. BOX 668
SAN MATEO, CALIF.

FRANCIS A. GUIDO
Editor-Publisher
Jack Gibson, John P. Carrick
Assistant Editors

Single Copy 50c

ROSTER OF EQUIPMENT
Monterey & Pacific Grove Railway

No.	1905 No.	1918 No.	Builder, Date
1	22	Scrapped	Fitzgerald, 1891
			Orig. horsecar, motorized, lengthened, dbl. trk., 1904-05
2	23	Scrapped	Fitzgerald, 1891
			Orig. horsecar, motorized, lengthened, dbl. trk., 1904-05
3	24	10	Fitzgerald, 1891
			Orig. horsecar, motorized, lengthened, dbl. trk., 1904-05
4	25	Scrapped	Fitzgerald, 1891
			Orig. horsecar, motorized, lengthened, dbl. trk., 1904-05
5	26	Scrapped	Fitzgerald, 1891
			Orig. horsecar, motorized, lengthened, dbl. trk., 1904-05
6	15	Scrapped	Fitzgerald, 1891
			Orig. horsecar, motorized, lengthened, dbl. trk., 1904-05
7	20	8	Fitzgerald, 1891
			Orig. horsecar, motorized, lengthened, dbl. trk., 1904-05
8	21	Scrapped	Fitzgerald, 1891
			Orig. horsecar, motorized, lengthened, dbl. trk., 1904-05
9	27	Scrapped	Fitzgerald, 1891
			Orig. horsecar, motorized, lengthened, dbl. trk., 1904-05
10	28	Scrapped	Fitzgerald, 1891
			Orig. horsecar, motorized, lengthened, dbl. trk., 1904-05
11	11	5	St. Louis Car. Co., 1904
			Orig. open motor car, rblt. to trlr. 1907; closed motor 1918
12	12	6	St. Louis Car. Co., 1904
			Orig. open motor car, rblt. to trlr. 1907; closed motor 1918
13	13	7	St. Louis Car. Co., 1904
			Orig. open motor car, rblt. to trlr. 1907; closed motor 1918
13	13	Linecar	M&PG Ry., 1904
			Orig. sgl. trk., lengthened & dbl. trk. (No number 1918)
14	14	9	St. Louis Car Co., 1904
			Orig. open motor car, rblt. to trlr. 1907; closed motor 1918
16	16	1	St. Louis Car Co., 1904
			Orig. combination motor. No change
17	17	2	St. Louis Car Co., 1904
			Orig. combination motor. No change
18	18	3	St. Louis Car Co., 1904
			Orig. combination motor. No change
19	19	4	St. Louis Car Co., 1904
			Orig. combination motor. No change
Del Monte			St. Louis Car. Co., 1905
			Orig. private parlor car. Later was used as sightseeing car

—Roster compiled by Erle C. Hanson from old records, State Railroad Commission and old timers of the era, 1953.

www.ingramcontent.com/pod-product-compliance
Lightning Source LLC
Chambersburg PA
CBHW031440040426
42444CB00006B/910